NATURE SERIES

GARDEN FLOWERS

By
JACQUELINE SEYMOUR

Designed by
DAVID GIBBON

Produced by
TED SMART

COOMBE BOOKS

First published in Great Britain 1978 by Colour Library International Ltd.,
Designed by David Gibbon. Produced by Ted Smart.
© Text: Jacqueline Seymour © Illustrations: CLI/Bruce Coleman Ltd.
Colour separations by La Cromolito, Milan, Italy.
Display and Text filmsetting by Focus Photoset, London, England.
Printed by I.G. Domingo and bound by Eurobinder, Barcelona (Spain)
All rights reserved.
ISBN No. 0 904681 42 4
COOMBE BOOKS

INTRODUCTION

We do not know what the first gardens were like, but it must have occurred to prehistoric man that, rather than travelling for long distances to forage for roots and berries, food plants could be grown in positions more convenient for him. No doubt he was sometimes unsuccessful in moving such plants but the advantages of having food close to his home, which could be harvested entirely for the benefit of himself and his family and protected from both human and animal marauders, would have made him persevere with his experimentation. As his knowledge and experience increased he would have also grown plants with magical and medicinal properties and perhaps even flowers for decoration. Lack of understanding of the chemistry and physiology of plant growth would eventually have led to impoverishment of the soil and resulted in shifting agriculture, still practised in some parts of the world today.

There is evidence that the ancient Egyptians understood and carried out techniques of cultivation along much the same lines as we do today. It is also known that they used cut flowers in vases for interior decoration as long ago as 2500 BC. The earliest surviving detailed garden plan is also Egyptian and dates from 1400 BC. It belonged to a high court official at Thebes and is of an elaborate and completely symmetrical design. Such sophistication must be evidence for a long history of garden design even by this early date.

The Greeks and Romans had gardens and used flowers for decoration and adornment but later, by early mediaeval times, there is little evidence for this kind of practice in Europe where most gardens belonged to monasteries and were largely devoted to growing herbs. The Renaissance saw a renewed interest in flowers and decoration became more studied and elaborate, garlands and wreaths being much in evidence in paintings of this time. Flowers were used at pageants and feasts as well as to decorate houses and churches. Varieties of garden flowers did not change very much until the nineteenth century when enormous advances occurred. The advent of the sailing clipper, which considerably reduced sailing time, meant that many exotic plants were introduced into Europe and the United States. There was also widespread interest in horticulture and botany resulting in increased knowledge which was used both to improve the old garden favourites and to grow the new foreign plants. Scientific advances also led to improved pest control. It has been suggested that the Industrial Revolution helped to stimulate the use of cut flowers because cheap vases and containers were then made available to all. The better and cheaper tools produced at this time would certainly have made the gardener's task an easier one. It is easy to see how and why the park-like landscape garden became less fashionable and how smaller gardens, full of masses of brilliant blooms, became common.

Gardening includes the art of grouping plants in visually satisfying arrangements but it is also a science, and, like any branch of science, it has its own special terminology or jargon. Some of these terms are easily understood by the layman; it is obvious that 'cultivar' is a portmanteau word for 'cultivated variety'. Other words are less easy to understand and are therefore defined in this text. On the other hand some familiar words take on a slightly different meaning when used by the specialist. For example a bulb, to a botanist, is specifically a modified underground shoot; for horticultural purposes bulbous plants include corms, tubers and rhizomes as well as bulbs. These are all underground food storage organs which have evolved as a method of surviving a long unfavourable season in a semi-dormant state and which are treated in very similar ways.

Frequent reference is made in this book to temperate and tropical regions. It is not possible to define such zones by lines of latitude, but temperate areas are generally taken to include all places where frost occurs in winter, even if this only happens rarely; altitude as well as latitude is an important factor. Most parts of Europe, the United States of America and parts of central Asia have a temperate climate; there plants are characterised by a winter resting season while tropical plants tend to grow continuously. The temperate climate is a particularly favourable one for the gardener; he can design his garden to include any or all of the following features: lawns, rose garden, rock garden, herbaceous border, annual border and woodland garden. Most of the great and famous gardens of the world are in temperate areas; the use of the lawn is probably the most noticeable difference between these gardens and those in the tropics and sub-tropics.

The gardener grows plants in places where they do not occur naturally and, by taking advantage of breeding programmes and selection, also grows plants which do not occur in wild communities. All our garden plants came from wild species; in some cases unusual types arose spontaneously and were deliberately propagated instead of the more usual varieties. This process has been especially significant in the history of cultivation of those flowers which have been grown for thousands of years like the rose and the lily. More recently, understanding of physiology, botany and genetics has allowed the horticulturalist to create hybrids with the object of obtaining larger flowers and fruit than those which have arisen naturally. Many of the garden flowers illustrated in this book are the results of breeding and selection by enthusiasts over very many years while others have not been deliberately changed by man and owe their beauty entirely to nature.

Facing page: Iceland Poppies.

3

Spring

Spring in the garden must surely always be associated in people's minds with the appearance of the first small and delicate flowers grown from bulbs. The Crocus *left* is one of the many easily grown hybrids. There are also autumn and winter flowering varieties; these often look their best in the rock garden. Among the earliest of all the spring flowers are Snowdrops *below left* and Winter Aconites (*Eranthis*) *far right*. Snowdrops, also known as Fair Maids of February, are easily naturalised as shown here. As its name suggests, Glory of the Snow (*Chionodoxa*) *near right* also blossoms early as does the very attractive windflower *Anemone blanda*. The blue-flowered form of this Anemone *below right* is the most common, but there are also pink, white and double varieties. The plants form rapidly-spreading clumps with feathery fern-like leaves.

Narcissi *left* and daffodils are the most commonly grown of all the spring bulbs. Today there are many hundreds of different kinds available, resulting from improvement and hybridisation from about twenty varieties which are know to have been in cultivation in Elizabethan times. *Narcissus* is the botanical name of the genus which includes both narcissi and daffodils, the distinction between them being that the name 'daffodil' is usually given to those flowers which have large trumpet-like centres and 'narcissus' to those with short cup-shaped centres. The popularity of these flowers is due not only to their attractive appearance but also to the fact that they are easily grown in a wide range of conditions; in addition they are extremely good for cutting.

Muscari *above* are also known as Grape or Musk Hyacinths. In Britain they appear in March or April, depending on the species. The Dog's Tooth Violet (*Erythronium*) *right,* sometimes known as the Trout Lily, is a European species which has heavily marbled leaves. There are a number of species native to North America many of which also have attractively patterned leaves.

7

Late Spring

Bulbocodium vernum is a member of the Lily family. Its rosy-purple flower *left* is very similar to that of the Autumn Crocus, although more funnel-shaped. Some botanists put them both in the same genus (*Colchicum*). The species can be found growing wild on mountain pastures throughout central Europe.

The *Euphorbia* genus is a huge one and its members range from succulents, trees and bushes to delicate herbaceous plants. The reason that these apparently dissimilar plants are grouped together is because they all possess an extremely unusual and specialised flower structure, known as a cyathium. The flowers are very small, several male flowers being grouped round a single female flower in the cup-shaped cyathium. Many Euphorbias have very showy leafy bracts as does *Euphorbia griffithi, below*. Here the bracts are red; the conspicuous yellow half-moon glands produce nectar.

The hardy and fragrant Lily of the Valley *right* is one of the prettiest of the smaller late spring flowers. The sturdier Tulip *below* is another garden favourite. The history of its cultivation is rather unusual. The genus is native to temperate Europe and Asia, the Middle East being particularly rich in species. Tulips have been grown in Turkish gardens for centuries; indeed the name itself is probably derived from the Turkish word meaning a turban. By the sixteenth century the tulip had become extremely fashionable in western Europe and in Holland tulip-growing spread to such an extent that it gave rise to the word 'tulipomania'. Huge sums of money were made and lost; single bulbs of new varieties changed hands for what now seem exorbitant prices. The Dutch government were eventually forced to intervene because the economy of the country itself was in jeopardy.

To this day the Dutch are the chief tulip producers in the world. About eight hundred varieties are commercially available but as many as three thousand cultivars are recognised. The range of colours and shapes is correspondingly large.

Spring Shrubs

There are a number of early-flowering shrubs which are particularly useful for bringing colour to the temperate garden. The Flowering Currant, which is a native of western North America, is an easily grown and very attractive example first introduced to Britain in the 1820s. The variety 'Pulborough Scarlet' *top left* is one of the best cultivars, freely producing deep red flowers.

Forsythia *below left*, also called Golden Bells, is another shrub which flowers early and before the appearance of its leaves. Forsythias are native to east Asia (except for one southern European species) and have been in cultivation for only one hundred and fifty years.

Unlike the Flowering Currant and Forsythia, which are deciduous, Rhododendrons are usually evergreen. The Rhododendron genus, which includes the Azaleas, is a large diverse one with over a thousand species and varieties which range from tiny bushes to large trees. Colours include pink *top right*, white, yellow, orange and red. The woodland garden at Scotney Castle, Kent, has Rhododendrons and Azaleas of many colours *below right*.

The Cottage Garden

'Cottage garden' conjures up a picture of unique charm which is essentially English—a small dwelling set in a mass of flowers. Such gardens became widespread in the nineteenth century; they were small in extent, full of flowering plants, and owed nothing to the earlier park-like landscape gardens which were not primarily for flowers. The cottager would have had little time to cultivate his flower garden, but many of the plants he grew were annuals which seeded themselves and to this extent the profusion of blossom may almost have been the result of neglect. Many varieties, now regarded as typically English, had in fact been brought from other parts of the world, particularly from warmer countries where the natural vegetation and flowers are much lusher and more vivid than those of temperate climates. The small modern flower garden is often designed on the same lines, and such flowers as Lupins, Daisies, Poppies, Pansies and Irises *left* are still favourites. Perhaps even more typical of the cottage garden are the Hollyhock *top right*, Sweet Pea *far right* and Honesty, of which the seedpods are shown *below*. Hollyhocks were introduced into cultivation in 1573, Honesty in 1595 and Sweet Peas are relative newcomers, being first imported from Sicily in 1699.

Love-in-a-Mist *left* is a hardy annual which has the ferny foliage typical of its genus, *Nigella,* and which has given rise to the common name of Fennel-flower. Love-in-a-Mist is also known as Devil-in-a-Bush, Jack-in-the-Green, Jack-in-Prison and Lady-in-the-Bower, names which probably all refer to the way the leaves surround the flower. The plant was introduced to Britain from southern Europe in 1570. The seed heads have an unusual shape and can be used for decoration when dried.

The star-like pale pink flowers of London Pride *below* are also old favourites. The plant earned its name because of its willingness to grow not only in the clean air of the country cottage garden but also in towns, tolerating the sooty and foggy atmosphere which used to be very much more prevalent than it is today. Years ago it was often seen bordering the paths which led to town houses, where its rosettes of evergreen leathery leaves formed a welcome touch of colour even in the darkest days of winter.

The Japanese Anemone is a flower of late summer and autumn whose beautiful blooms are borne on long stems. One is shown here *right* with the caterpillar of an Angle Shades Moth walking over it.

Yellow Loosestrife *below* is a hardy herbaceous perennial introduced from southern Europe in 1820. Although in its natural state it prefers damp places, it will grow and spread rapidly in most situations. Its popularity in old gardens may be because it had a reputation for stopping bleeding and checking fever. The plant also yields a yellow dye.

16

No cottage garden would have been complete without the traditional ramblers, the 'roses round the door', as well as rose bushes amongst the other flowers. These were not the hybrid tea and floribunda roses which are so familiar today, but would have been varieties now listed in catalogues as 'Old Fashioned Roses' including such favourites as Moss Roses, Cabbage Roses, and those known as Polyantha or Pom-pom Roses. The modern gardener is fortunate in being able to grow these beautiful, sometimes heavily scented, flowers and he can also enjoy the work of more recent breeders, examples of which are illustrated. 'Gustave Frahm' *far left* is a robust-looking floribunda rose. 'Michelle Meilland' *near left*, a particularly pretty shade of pink, is a hybrid tea rose, as is 'Piccadilly' *below left*.

Hardy annual plants are easy to grow and extremely popular because they produce a brilliant display of flowers remarkably quickly. An annual is a plant which completes its life cycle within a year and then dies. Annuals therefore rely on their seeds to produce new plants and are, of course, always grown from seed, but in different environments such plants may behave differently. Plants which grow as annuals in colder regions may be perennial in habit in less extreme climates. In the wild, two kinds of annuals can be distinguished, summer annuals and winter annuals. This division is entirely related to climate. Summer annuals germinate in the spring, flower in the summer and die at the beginning of winter and are found in places where the winters are cold. Winter annuals germinate in the autumn, grow through the winter, flower in the spring and die in the summer as a result of heat and drought. From a cultural point of view it is always useful to know the origin of any given species as this will give some idea of the conditions that the plant will or will not withstand.

Nasturtiums *top right* are sometimes known as Indian Cress, presumably because of the hot taste of the leaves, which can be used in salads. The species most often cultivated, *Tropaeolum majus*, comes from Peru and is an annual climber although some of the cultivars are dwarf non-climbing forms.

Lobelia erinus, bottom right, is an annual originating from South Africa which was first introduced into cultivation in Britain in 1752. There are perennial species as well but they all come from warmer parts of the world and are therefore treated as annuals in temperate regions.

More Annuals

The Garden Mallow (*Lavatera*) is a tall annual plant with large rose-pink flowers which grows to over a metre high, rather taller than most annuals grown in British gardens. It is a close relative of the Hollyhock. Another related genus, very similar in appearance, is *Sidalcea*. The flowers *left* of this perennial are very like those of perennial mallows of the genera *Malva* and *Lavatera*.

The Tobacco Plant (*Nicotiana*) is named after a French Consul in Portugal, Jean Nicot, who introduced it to France and Portugal. The large-flowered variety *right* is purely ornamental. The sweet scent of the flowers is most noticeable in the evening and attracts moths which pollinate the flowers. The Tobacco Plant is grown as an annual in temperate regions.

Members of the *Helipterum* genus are known as everlasting flowers or immortelles because they retain their colour after being dried. They are half-hardy annuals much used as cut flowers. Double varieties of *Helipterum roseum, below,* are marketed under the name of *Acroclinium*.

Bedding Plants

Temporary occupants of flower beds are known as bedding plants; nearly all of them are grown in a nursery bed or greenhouse before being planted or 'bedded out'. They are usually annuals or plants which, by virtue of the climate, are treated as annuals. Such plants include Lobelias and Tobacco Plants, illustrated previously, and the plants shown here. Tender perennial plants like Fuchsias can also be used for bedding but are returned to the shelter of the greenhouse for the winter. Spring bedding schemes often include such bulbs as Tulips and Hyacinths.

Nemesias *far left* and Toadflax *near left* both have annual and perennial forms; those illustrated here are annuals suitable for summer display. The genus *Tagetes* includes the flowers known as French Marigolds and African Marigolds, but these are misleading names as the species from which they were bred come from Mexico. Both these Marigolds are sun-loving annuals. The variety called 'Paprika' is shown *below left*.

The Petunia *top right* is another popular bedding plant. It is a native of Central and South America and, because it is only half-hardy in cooler regions, it too is treated as an annual. Similarly Antirrhinums or Snapdragons *bottom right* are usually treated as half-hardy annuals although they are in fact perennials. They are also grown for cut flowers, particularly in the United States. The flower of the Antirrhinum is not unlike the snout of a dragon; pinching and releasing the sides causes the dragon's jaws to open and close.

21

Butterfly and Bee Plants

Many people, even if they are not bee-keepers, like to grow plants which attract bees and other insects. Visitors such as the Red Admiral Butterfly *left*, here seen feeding on Red Valerian flowers, add to the interest of any garden. The other plants pictured on these pages are also particularly attractive to insects.

Michaelmas Daisies flower late in the summer and provide a source of pollen and nectar for bees and other insects at the end of the season; those *below* have a hoverfly feeding on them. Perhaps the best known of all such plants is the Buddleia *near right* which is also known as the Butterfly Bush. It has an excellent honey flow extremely attractive to bees as well as to butterflies. The Eryngium *far right* is a close relative of sea holly. It is valuable as a foliage plant and is worth drying for winter flower arrangements although the prickles make it difficult to handle. Sweet Williams *bottom right* are perennials which, because they deteriorate rapidly after the second year, are usually grown as biennials.

The relationship between wild plants and insects which visit them is a mutually beneficial one. The insects collect pollen and nectar, which they use as food, but in so doing they transfer pollen from the male parts of the flower to the female parts, so effecting pollination. This enables seeds to develop and allows the plant to reproduce itself. The flower consists not only of the male and female reproductive parts of the plant but also of showy, often brightly coloured, petals (or sepals) which attract pollinators which can be butterflies or moths, bees, other insects or birds. Some plants, like the grasses, have inconspicuous flowers but they do not rely on insects for pollination. Most garden flowers have an attractive colourful structure but some of them depend on the gardener and not on insects for reproduction. This is often because inbreeding has resulted in sterile forms–some hydrangeas are a case in point–or because cultivation has removed the plant from its pollinator. For example, in the wild, Yuccas are pollinated by a particular kind of moth not found anywhere but in central America where these plants grow. So, if seeds are desired, the plant has to be pollinated by hand when grown in any other part of the world. The gardener may also bring about vegetative propagation by taking cuttings, rooting runners, dividing clumps of plants, or grafting.

Hebes are members of a genus of shrubs most of which are natives of New Zealand. They are evergreens and the flowers appear in dense spikes in high summer and autumn. They were formerly placed in the *Veronica* genus and many gardeners still know them by that name. The variety shown *top left* is called 'Miss E. Fittall'.

Lilac (*Syringa*) *bottom left* attracts insects mainly by its strong scent, whereas *Sedum spectabile* presents a large flat attractive area of colour easy for an insect to alight on. This succulent originally came from China; the cultivar *right* is called 'Carmen'.

Sunlovers

A number of garden flowers are noted for their willingness, indeed their need, to grow in hot sunny positions. Many of these are daisies and many of them originate from South Africa. Gazanias *top left*, also known as Treasure Flowers, only open in the sun and, whatever the weather, are closed by mid-afternoon.

Venidio-arctotis *far left* is one of a number of artificial hybrids between the *Venidium* and *Arctotis* genera. These hybrids were created in England and some have remained fertile and can be grown from seed. The parents are both native to South Africa. *Arctotheca calendula, below,* is another South African daisy, photographed in its native country. The Giant Sunflower *far right* is an old favourite, particularly with children. It is of economic importance as the seeds are used to feed birds and produce an edible oil; the flowers yield a yellow dye.

There are a number of species and many varieties of annual Chrysanthemum *near right*; most of the species come from the continent of Africa. Mesembryanthemums *bottom right* are South African succulents also known as Ice Plants. Although they look as though they too belong to the daisy family (Compositae) they are not related, being members of the Aizoaceae.

Gardens
in the Sun

Plants native to temperate regions rarely take kindly to tropical climates but to the Briton living abroad such plants bring welcome reminders of home. This garden *top left* at Subukia in the Kenya Highlands could have been created by such a person. Close inspection reveals plants typical of the English garden such as Foxgloves, Lavender and Water Lilies. Yet the whole scene is quite un-English, dominated as it is by the dramatically beautiful and typically African Acacia trees.

The Spanish Bayonet *below* is a Yucca, native to east Mexico, which grows out of doors in the sub-tropics in other parts of the world. Like the Gloxinia *bottom right*, another species from South America, it is too tender to grow out of doors in cooler regions where it has to be cultivated as a house or greenhouse plant. A typically Mediterranean plant is the Oleander *top right*. Most oleanders are pink-flowered shrubs; this white one was photographed in Spain.

The Common Trumpet Creeper or Trumpet Vine *left* is a deciduous climber brought from south-east America in the early seventeenth century. It climbs by using aerial roots, like ivy, and is particularly common in the Mediterranean region. The Hibiscus or Rose Mallow *right* is another common plant of this area. There are about one hundred and fifty species of *Hibiscus* including herbs, shrubs and small trees.

The Poinsettia *below* is another member of the *Euphorbia* genus. The bright red 'petals' are large and unusually showy bracts. Poinsettias can be seen in flower all the year round in equatorial regions, where daylight always lasts for about twelve hours and yet they only flower in midwinter in Trinidad. This is because they are what is called 'short day' plants; they make their growth when the days are long and are only stimulated to flower when the days are appropriately short. Other plants will only produce flowers after being stimulated by a period of low temperature. These and similar factors are often the reasons why plants native to temperate regions cannot be persuaded to grow satisfactorily in hotter gardens.

The Herbaceous Border

The herbaceous border is filled with plants which grow harmoniously together and give long periods of colour from spring to autumn. Plants known as 'herbaceous' have a life span of more than two years but they die down each autumn and produce new growth the following spring. Originally the herbaceous border contained only plants of this kind but today the border is often 'mixed' and includes bulbs, annuals, shrubs and roses. Many plants are naturally herbaceous like those illustrated here. Others are herbaceous in habit when cut back in the autumn by frost. Cranesbills (*Geranium*) are hardy summer-flowering plants; this one *left* is the Iberian Cranesbill.

The shape of the flowers of *Dicentra spectabilis, below,* has given rise to some unusual common names: Lyre Flower, Bleeding Heart, Lady-in-the-Bath, Lady's Locket and Dutchman's Breeches. White and pink Delphiniums can be obtained as well as the more usual blues and mauves. This variety *right* is 'Blue Jade'.

The Hostas or Plantain Lilies *far left* come from Japan. Formerly known as Funkias (after a Dr. Funk), they have attractive foliage popular with flower arrangers and are useful where ground cover is needed. There are thirty or so different varieties to choose from with leaves varying in colour and pattern. The flowers form rather subdued spikes of purple, lilac and white.

Torch Lilies or Red Hot Pokers *near left* are popular perennials for the border. They come from South Africa and like sun and light soil; once planted they should not be disturbed. They flower in late summer. In contrast, Columbines (*Aquilegia*) flower early in the summer and do not like full sun. They are available in a wide range of colours and the modern long-spurred hybrids *bottom left* are a particularly charming addition to the flower garden.

There are a number of different kinds of Cornflower in cultivation, but the hardy perennial *top right* is usually chosen for the border.

Yarrow or Sneezewort (*Achillea*) has flat flowerheads attractive to butterflies. The dried heads are suitable for winter flower arrangements. There are a number of golden cultivars: 'Coronation Gold' *bottom right* grows to about one metre high, but some ar taller and suitable for the back of the border; dwarf and spreading varieties are suitable for the rock garden. They all flower in late summer.

Erigeron glaucus, overleaf top left, has large lavender-coloured daisy-like flowers which last well in water. The blue cornflower-like flowers of Cupid's Dart (*Catananche*) *overleaf bottom left* are also good for cutting. They are semi-everlasting, and have thin dry translucent bracts which give the undersides a silvery appearance. The plant has been in cultivation since the end of the sixteenth century and probably came originally from the Mediterranean. It is also known as Blue Cupidone, another name which is derived from the fact that it is reputed to have been used in love potions.

Coneflowers (*Rudbeckia*) *overleaf right* come from North America. The genus, which includes the Black-eyed Susan, was named by the botanist Linnaeus after a Swedish family in which he once held the post of tutor. The father, Professor Olaf Rudbeck, was a botanist whose counsel Linnaeus valued very highly. There are a number of varieties of *Rudbeckia* in cultivation, many of which, although really perennial in habit, are more usually grown today as annuals. In general they like a sunny well-drained position.

35

Iceland Poppies (*page 2*) and Oriental Poppies *above left* are both perennial plants although the Iceland Poppy, which was introduced from arctic regions in 1759, is usually treated as an annual or biennial. It is the only poppy generally considered to be worth cutting. The larger Oriental Poppies are favourite plants for the herbaceous border.

Part of the appeal of Pansies *below* must surely be their little round faces with whisker-like markings. They are used mainly for summer bedding and are usually treated as biennials.

The delicate Gypsophila or Chalk Plant prefers chalky soils and is a favourite with flower arrangers. *Gypsophila paniculata* is also known as Baby's Breath or Gauze Plant, the cultivar illustrated *top right* is called 'Rosy Veil'. All these names indicate the airiness and grace of the plant and its flowers. Another good cut flower is Great Masterwort (*Astrantia*) *bottom right*. The flowers themselves are rather insignificant but they are surrounded by conspicuous papery bracts.

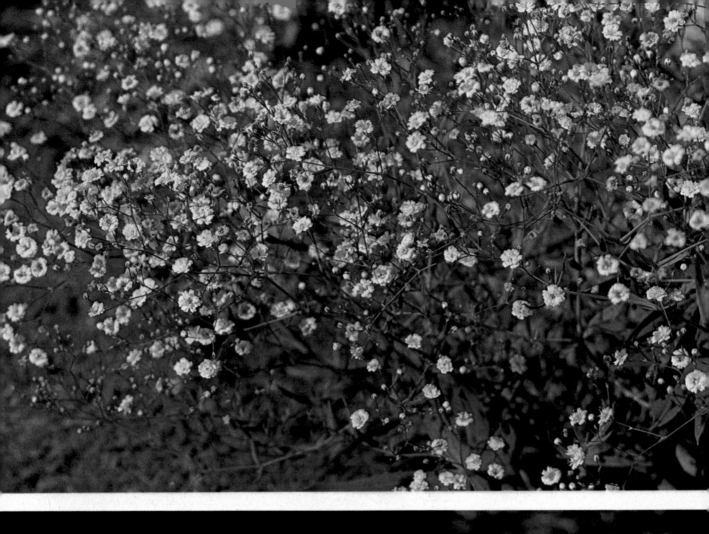

Biennials

Biennials are plants which do not flower during their first season of growth. The gardener therefore sows his seeds one year, the plants flower the following year and then, if true biennials, they die. Advantages of such plants are that they are put out into their flowering position in the autumn, so easing the work load in the spring, and they come into bloom earlier than the annuals which are not planted until the spring. A disadvantage is the space they take up before being planted-out into their final positions.

Honesty *left* is a biennial; the seed pods, already illustrated, are particularly useful for winter decoration indoors. There are about forty wild species of Forget-me-not *below*, mostly from Europe and Australia; these include annuals, biennials and perennials.

The Foxglove *right* is a biennial or short-lived perennial from east and central Asia. Its leaves are the source of a poisonous drug used to control heart rate although nowadays the natural product has been largely superseded by synthetic ones.

Climbers and Wall Plants

There is widespread disagreement about how the name of the climber shown *left* should be spelt. It was named after a Professor Caspar Wistar who was of German descent, the family name originally being Wüster. This name had been altered and one branch of the family called themselves Wistar; the other was known as Wister. Thomas Nuttall, who named the genus spelt the Professor's name Wistar but the plant's *Wisteria*. Both versions are commonly found in books. Sweet Wisteria *left* is a hardy deciduous climber introduced from China.

Chaenomeles japonica, the Japanese Flowering Quince, *below* was formerly known as *Cydonia*, a name which is still in common use. It is often inexactly referred to as Japonica. As this is an adjective, which simply means 'Japanese', used as the specific name of many other plants imported from Japan, such usage can cause confusion.

There are at least two hundred species of *Clematis*. 'Barbara Dibley' *right* is a large free-flowering hybrid.

The Water Garden

The water garden is a very old form of garden. It is known that the Egyptians grew water lilies *left* as long ago as 2000 BC. Japanese water gardens are deservedly well-known and have been for many centuries. In Europe and North America water gardens range from formal pools to ponds surrounded by damp areas suitable for moisture-loving plants. Many water plants dislike running water and water lilies in particular will not grow successfully in a strong current or even near a dripping fountain. They do, however, all need to have their roots in water; the depth necessary depends on the variety being grown. Water Lilies are shown in a formal water garden *below* at Hidcote Manor, Gloucestershire. The gardens at Hidcote were designed by the American gardener Lawrence Johnston.

The Irises make up a large group of plants of very different characteristics. The blue *Iris laevigata, right,* is quite happy growing in a few inches of water at the edge of a pond or in the moist soil surrounding it. Other kinds are suited to a well-drained soil and do very well in a herbaceous border. Other familiar plants which grow well in and around the edges of ponds are Willows and Marsh Marigolds, both shown in flower *below.* This is the double-flowered form of the Marsh Marigold; its other names are Native Kingcup and Water Cowslip.

The damp or boggy area round an informal pool or pond is a favourable environment for the moisture-loving plants pictured here. The Trollius or Globe Flower is an early-flowering plant with large buttercup-like flowers which likes such cool wet places. There are a number of species of *Trollius,* all hardy perennials and all native to northern temperate and arctic regions; they have given rise to some good cultivars *left.*

The Monkey Flower or Monkey Musk *below* is another hardy perennial which likes moisture. The markings on the flowers were thought to resemble a monkey's face, hence the name. The plant can also be grown in rock gardens.

The feathery plumes of the Astilbe or False Goatsbeard *right* are composed of masses of tiny flowers. The plant will grow in semi-shade, flowering in midsummer. It also makes an attractive pot plant.

The Herb Garden

There are almost as many different kinds of herb garden as there are gardeners. Nowadays such a garden can range from a few basic culinary herbs, such as parsley, mint and sage, to large collections of plants, some of which have been used medicinally in the past. Frequently such plants have aromatic foliage and can be used to advantage to make a scented garden.

There are numerous garden varieties of Bergamot or Bee Balm. 'Cambridge Scarlet' *far left* is an example and there are others with pink or white flowers. Bergamot is a member of the mint family and in North America was made into Oswego Tea, probably first used by the Red Indians both as a drink and as a treatment for bronchitis. Lemon Balm *near left* is another member of the mint family, and, like Bergamot, is a favourite with bees. Its scientific name *Melissa* is the Greek for bee and the belief that bees will never desert a hive if balm grows nearby has been current for centuries.

Members of the mallow family have been used for the treatment of all kinds of ills and are said to have a soothing effect. *Malope*, an annual herb from Spain, is a member of this family. Its large flowers *bottom left* can bring a welcome splash of colour to the herb garden.

Lavender has never been much used medicinally but has been valued as a source of perfume from at least as early as Roman times. The name comes from *lavare*, to wash, and it is known that the Romans used it as a bath perfume. Of the best modern cultivars the dwarf shrub 'Hidcote' *top right* has the deepest blue flowers.

Thyme *centre right* is one of the basic culinary herbs. It is especially useful for growing in the rock garden, in crevices between paving stones or between bricks edging a border. Thyme is very attractive to bees; the honey produced when they have access to a large number of flowers is considered to be particularly good. Sage is another widely-used culinary herb but, unlike thyme, it has also been used medicinally for hundreds of years. The uses to which it was put were numerous and varied, as was so often the case with medicinal herbs. There are many cultivars in the genus (*Salvia*) including the familiar red-flowered bedding plants. The example shown here *bottom right, Salvia* x *superba,* is an ornamental hardy herbaceous plant and not a culinary variety.

49

Foliage

Plants with unusual foliage have a special place in the garden for they provide patches of colour for a longer season than those plants which are grown solely for the beauty of their flowers.

Many forms of *Coleus* are grown for their unusually coloured leaves. Jacob's Coat *left* comes from south-east Asia and, like other members of its genus, it is grown as a house or greenhouse plant in temperate regions. *Euphorbia marginata, right,* is a half-hardy annual from the United States also known as Ghost Weed or Snow on the Mountains. It has striped leaves and bracts.

The creeping evergreen Periwinkle *Vinca major* 'Variegata' makes an excellent ground cover and also has a long flowering season, blooming from late spring to early autumn. It is shown *below* with the flowers of an everlasting daisy (*Helichrysum*) known as the Curry Plant.

Shrubs

Shrubs are perennial woody plants, differing from trees in that they branch from the base and do not have a single main stem; like trees they can be deciduous or evergreen. Shrub gardening has increased in popularity in the last twenty-five years. Compared with many other plants, shrubs need little attention, an important factor in their favour for the busy modern gardener, but they can provide as brilliant colours and heady scents as their herbaceous relatives. Roses are shrubs; some have already been illustrated in the section on cottage gardens.

The evergreen Escallonia *top left* comes from Chile and Brazil and prefers a sunny position. Hydrangeas are deciduous and will grow in sun or shade; they come from north America and Asia. The large flower-head of a Hydrangea is made up of a number of small flowers or florets. Sometimes these florets can be seen to be of two distinct types; there are larger ones round the outside, which are sterile, and smaller, fertile ones in the centre. The familiar Mophead type of Hydrangea *bottom left* is made up entirely of the larger sterile florets; the flatter flower-head of the so-called Lacecap Hydrangea is composed of both types. The colour of the Hydrangea varies with the soil on which it is grown; it is pink or red on alkaline soils such as those containing a lot of lime, but is blue on acidic, peaty soils.

One of the many different varieties of Fuchsia is shown *far right*. In the wild the coloured sepals are usually red and the petals making up the corolla are purple, but cultivars come in all shades and combinations of pink, red and purple. Fuchsias were extremely fashionable in the Victorian era, reaching a peak of popularity in the 1880s.

Mock Orange (*Philadelphus*) *near right* is often mistakenly called Syringa, which is the botanical name of the Lilac genus. This confusion is not of recent origin and probably dates from the sixteenth century when both the Mock Orange and the Lilac were introduced at the same time to the Austrian court from Turkey.

The habit of shrubby plants varies considerably; the Fuchsia is a small low-growing shrub whereas the Mock Orange can reach the height of a small tree and *Solanum crispum, bottom right,* is a vigorous climber growing to a height of five metres or so. The bluish-purple flowers reveal its kinship with the potato, tomato and nightshades, all of which are near relatives.

Fossil remains of Magnolias over five million years old have been found; they are considered by botanists to be one of the most primitive of flowering plants. The genus is composed of about eighty species of shrubs and trees, some evergreen, some deciduous, many of which are cultivated for their large and beautiful flowers like those of the Yulan or Lily Tree *left*.

The Cistus or Rock Rose *below* and the Broom *right* are colourful and decorative shrubs. Cistuses, natives of southern Europe and northern Africa, are not generally hardy; Brooms are not long-lived and become straggly and untidy in their old age. Both are valuable for their attractive blossom—the fragile saucer-shaped blooms of the Cistus and the showers of pea-like flowers of the Broom.

The Rock Garden

A rock garden should be designed to look as if it is a natural part of a rocky hillside or slope; it is often a good way of coping with the problem of a steep bank or of making an attractive and convenient transition between different levels of a garden. Many of the plants grown in the rock garden are technically alpines, a botanical term which refers to plants which grow only between the permanent snow line and the limit of conifer tree growth.

The Pasque Flower *below right*, as its name suggests, flowers around Easter time. It is an alpine, like *Phlox subulata, top left.* This forms a mat which, in spring, is smothered in white, mauve or pink flowers. Purple Rock-cress, *Aubrieta, right* is another spring-flowering perennial plant with a more trailing habit than the Phlox.

Campanulas or Bellflowers, like Phlox, are familiar plants of the herbaceous border, but dwarf forms like *Campanula carpatica, bottom left,* bring summer colour to the rock garden.

Summer Bulbs

There are a large number of varieties of bulbs available which are suitable for growing to flower in the summer; the range is such that it is possible to find bulbs suitable for any soil or position in the garden. They include, using the word bulb in its horticultural sense, Anemones, Begonias, Dahlias, Freesias, Gladioli, Montbretias and Irises, but the most popular of all are the lilies of the genus *Lilium,* hybrids of which are illustrated. Like the rose, the lily has been grown and cherished for thousands of years. We know that the lily was used by the Pharaohs in their funeral wreaths; since the early Middle Ages it has been particularly associated with the Virgin Mary.

Although the lily has been cultivated for such a long time it is still being improved. Significant advances have been made in the last thirty years with the development of large-flowered hybrids, many of which have beautiful scents. These lilies are hardy and disease-resistant with large and beautiful flowers like those of the Golden-rayed Lily hybrid *left,* Tiger Lily hybrid *right* and Mid-Century hybrid 'Enchantment' *below.*

Autumn

Sneezeweed (*Helenium*) is a late-flowering herbaceous plant; its colours range through dark reds and browns to yellow. The genus is named after Helen of Troy for, according to legend, the flowers sprang from her tears. 'Moerheim Beauty' *far right* is a good cultivar.

Dahlias bloom first in late summer and continue flowering until the autumn frosts. They are only half-hardy and the tuberous roots have to be lifted and dried for the winter. They are classified by the shape of the flower; a red pompom *near right* and a yellow single variety *bottom right* are shown. Like Dahlias, Chrysanthemums have been the subjects of extensive breeding programmes and are available in many different forms, sizes and colours. The Japanese Chrysanthemums are the most varied and elaborate of them all and come in a wide range of colours. A yellow double variety is shown *below*.

The plants mentioned above are all members of the daisy family; the Geum belongs to the rose family. 'Red Wings' *left* is a late-flowering cultivar of *Geum chiloense*.

Winter

Plants which flower in winter in temperate zones are usually derived from wild forms native to colder areas of the world. Three yellow-flowered shrubs which all originally came from China are Jasmine *left*, *Mahonia japonica*, *right*, and Witch Hazel *far right*.

Winter Jasmine is a deciduous sprawling shrub which can be grown as a climber if attached to suitable supports. The flowers appear in late winter and early spring and have no scent, unlike those of the *Mahonia* which have a smell reminiscent of Lily of the Valley. *Mahonia* is a genus of evergreens related to the *Berberis*.

Chinese Witch Hazel is very hardy and easily grown; in favourable conditions this deciduous shrub reaches the height of a small tree. The flowers have an unusual shape and scent; both flowers and fruit can be seen on the plant at the same time.

The Christmas Rose *below* is not always in flower in Britain for Christmas, but first blooms appear soon afterwards. It is, of course, not a true rose but a member of the buttercup family. The delicate-looking flowers are long-lasting; some gardeners like to cover them to protect them against the dirty winter weather.

INDEX

Page numbers refer to illustrations.